Little Johnny's Faith Adventures

Our Beginnings

Jacqui Wilson

WestBow
PRESS
A DIVISION OF THOMAS NELSON

Photographs by Sonya Rudolph

WestBow Press books may be ordered through booksellers or by contacting:

WestBow Press
A Division of Thomas Nelson
1663 Liberty Drive
Bloomington, IN 47403
www.westbowpress.com
1-(866) 928-1240

ISBN: 978-1-4497-0790-3 (sc)
ISBN: 978-1-4497-0667-8 (e)

Library of Congress Control Number: 2010939291

Printed in the United States of America

WestBow Press rev. date: 12/3/2010

To God for calling me "out of darkness into the marvelous light" and for allowing me to serve in this Great Commission given by Jesus.

Contents

Preface

In the summer of 2009, my church's Wednesday Night Bible Study program needed a teacher for the age group seven and below. As a favor, I volunteered to be the temporary teacher. However, temporary continues, and the young group has become known as the Rockland M. B. Church Son Shiners.

During the first year, I discovered two very important facts. First, teaching young children is my calling from God. Before I knew my purpose in life, God had already laid the foundation I needed to take on this endeavor. I come from a family of Christian educators, and I have a natural ability to be creative and organized. This book is the result. It consists of four stories about little Johnny and his daily adventures followed by the bible lessons little Johnny learns. Second, these young souls have the ability to learn and to apply God's word. Since the inception of the Son Shiners, they have ministered and blessed the souls of so many people by expressing their knowledge of the bible and singing. I am truly making a difference. You can make a difference. My goal and hope is that this book will help parents and teachers equip their children to deal with the daily challenges in the manner God wants. This truly is the best investment you can ever make in a child's life. Proverbs 22:6 (KJV) states, "Train up a child in the way he should go: and when he is old, he will not depart from it." This is your opportunity.

~Acknowledgments~

~To my Grandmother, Eva Crusoe Smith, I am truly grateful for the foundation of ministry and education you have laid for our family. Your dedication to children in the church and the community has given me such an awesome legacy to fulfill.

~To Doricia Crawford, Elder Henry Crawford, Kimberly Crawford, Joan Hirsch, Minister John Hirsch, and Sharon Love, I cannot express my momentous gratitude for your support in this endeavor.

~To the Rockland Missionary Baptist Church Son Shiners, this started with you. You will always hold a special place in my heart.

~To my Aunt Juanita Stork-Williams, who started her flight to heaven, thank you for the unconditional love you gave to everyone. We will see you again some day.

~To all my family and friends, you have supported me and inspired me in so many ways. Thank you and I love you.

STORIES SYNOPSES

"Little Johnny Discovers God's Creation" Have you ever wondered who made the birds and the bees or the trees and the seas? Little Johnny did. With his grandpa's help, little Johnny learns how God created the whole world and receives a daily reminder of God's great work. Lesson 1 God Created Everything

"Little Johnny and God's Breath" In this delightful story, little Johnny discovers how God made the first man and woman. Little Johnny is super excited when his grandpa demonstrates God's awesomeness using dough. Lesson 2 God Created Adam and Eve

"Little Johnny and the Football Fiasco" Little Johnny and his friend Jimmy find themselves in a sticky situation when they are disobedient. The end result is a damaged flower bed, a broken window, and a $150 bill. Travel into this story with little Johnny as he learns about the consequences of being disobedient. Lesson 3 Happy Face or Sad Face

"Little Johnny and the Big Gold Star" In this story, little Johnny doesn't do his best and becomes jealous of his friend, Jimmy, who gets the big gold star. As a result of his anger, Johnny loses his friend, but later discovers how to get past being mad. Lesson 4 God Wants Your Best and Lesson 5 Be Mad, But Don't Do Wrong

Little Johnny
Discovers
God's Creation

One night, little Johnny sat on the porch with his grandpa looking at the stars above. As they searched the stars, little Johnny pointed and asked, "Grandpa who made that big star right there?"

Grandpa simply answered, "God."

Little Johnny pondered what his grandpa said and then asked, "What about the star right there?" as he pointed far east.

With a smile on his face, Grandpa simply answered, "God."

As little Johnny prepared for bed that night, he asked, "Grandpa what about the stars I see out of my window at night?"

Still smiling, Grandpa simply answered, "God."

The next morning little Johnny and his grandpa went to the park to play. As they walked through the park toward the playground, little Johnny asked, "Grandpa, who made the trees?"

Grandpa simply answered "God." With that answer, little Johnny took off to play. Oh, he had so much fun at the park. He played in the grass and climbed the trees. He smelled the flowers and even chased bees.

On their way home from the park, little Johnny and his grandpa passed by a huge lake. Several people were fishing and riding in BIG sailboats. Little Johnny turned to his grandpa with full round eyes and asked, "Grandpa, who made the lakes and the fish?"

Grandpa looked down at little Johnny and said, "You already know the answer to that question Johnny. The answer is God." Bending down and looking little Johnny directly in the eye, Grandpa said, "I think it's time for you to learn how everything was made. How about this? After dinner tonight, you and I will read about it."

"Really! I can't wait!" exclaimed little Johnny, jumping up and down.

That night, Grandma made little Johnny's favorite meal, but little Johnny hardly noticed. So excited to FINALLY know who made everything, little Johnny just gobbled down his meal, and Grandpa simply chuckled.

As soon as Grandpa completed his meal, little Johnny jumped from his seat. "Ok, Grandpa. It's time." Laughing, Grandpa said, "Johnny, we will read the story, but first you must complete your evening chores. While you complete your chores, I will prepare everything."

Curious, little Johnny asked, "What's everything?"

"You will see," Grandpa replied, walking into the family room.

Little Johnny hurried to clear the dinner table and sweep the floor. As he cleaned, little Johnny took peeks to see what his grandpa did. Grandpa gathered two pieces of paper. One piece of paper was black and the other white. Also, little Johnny saw his grandpa gather a hole puncher, glue stick, string, and crayons. Little Johnny wrinkled his face in wonder.

"Why does Grandpa need those things," little Johnny thought to himself, "after all, they were just reading a book." Grandpa passed near the dining room door, but little Johnny jumped back before grandpa could catch him peeking.

Finally, "Johnny," his grandpa called.

"Yes sir!"

"Are you ready?"

"Yes sir!" exclaimed little Johnny. Immediately, little Johnny put the broom in place and rushed into the family room and sat in his favorite spot.

Grandpa sat in his big comfortable chair and pulled out his big black bible. Little Johnny would recognize his grandpa's bible anywhere. Every Sunday, his grandpa would have the bible tucked underneath his arm. Grandpa always said, "Johnny, this is my tool for life." And little Johnny always wondered how the bible was a tool. "You couldn't use it like a hammer. Could you?" he would think.

Grandpa said, "I know you are wondering why I have my bible and these school supplies. These will help me tell the story of God's creation." Slowly, Grandpa opened his bible and began to read. "In the beginning God created the heavens and the earth." Grandpa picked up the black paper and said, "And darkness was in the deep. God said let there be light and there was light." Grandpa picked up the white paper. "God saw that the light was a good thing. Then, God divided the light from the darkness." Grandpa glued the white paper and the black paper back to back. "Johnny, what do you think God called the light?"

"Day!"

"And the dark?"

"Night!"

"And the evening and morning were the first day. Now, water covered the entire Earth. So, God decided to divide the water. God placed some water up top." Grandpa raised his hands. "And God decided to put some water at the bottom." Grandpa lowered his hands. "Johnny, do you know how God divided the water?"

"How Grandpa?"

"God placed Heaven in between." Johnny's eyes got really big as he curiously watched his grandpa draw clouds on the white paper. "And the evening and morning were the second day. Next, God said let all the water under Heaven gather in one place and let the dry land appear. And it happened. God called the dry land Earth and the water Seas." Grandpa drew a body of water on one side of the paper and brown land on the other side. Grandpa turned the picture to little Johnny and said, "And God saw that it was a good thing. But! God did not stop there. God said to the earth bring forth grass, flowers, and fruit trees. And the Earth did." Grandpa drew grass, a tree, and some flowers. Grandpa showed little Johnny the picture and said, "God saw that it was a good thing. And the evening and morning were the third day."

Grandpa went on, "Now God had created the Earth, the Heaven, the trees, and the seas, but there were some things still missing. Johnny, what tells us when it is daytime?"

"Grandpa, that's easy—the Sun."

"And what tells us when it is night time?"

"The moon and stars Grandpa."

Grandpa pulled out the yellow crayon and drew the Sun on the white side and the moon and stars on the black side. "Johnny, God gave us the Sun, moon, and stars, so we would have signs, seasons, days, and years. And you know what… God saw that it was.…"

Interrupting, "A good thing!" exclaimed Johnny.

Grandpa chuckled and said, "And the evening and morning were the fourth day. But! God was not done yet. He told the waters to bring forth the fish, great whales, and other sea animals. Also, God created the birds to fly in Heaven." Grandpa drew a bird in the air and a fish in the Sea. He followed with, "And the evening and morning were the fifth day. After creating the birds and fish, God still was not done. Next, God created some oink oinks."

"Pigs!" exclaimed Johnny. And Grandpa drew it.

"Woof woofs"

"Dogs!" exclaimed Johnny. And Grandpa drew it.

"Moo moos"

"Cows!" exclaimed Johnny. And Grandpa drew it.

"And some ROARS!"

Giggling little Johnny shouted, "Lions and Bears!"

"Yes! God created all the animals that roam the Earth. But you know what Johnny, God still was not done. He had one more very special project. It was the most special project of all. Do you know what it was? God made a man like you and me, and He made the woman." Grandpa drew a man and a woman.

"God looked at everything He had made and it was very good. And the evening and morning were the sixth day. On the seventh day, God sanctified it and rested. So, Johnny the answer to all your questions of who made everything is…."

"God!" exclaimed little Johnny.

Grandpa picked up the picture and punched a hole in the very top. Then, Grandpa took the piece of string, put it through the hole, and tied a knot to make a loop. "This is for you Johnny. Hang it on your bedroom door. At night, flip it to the black side, and remember God made the moon and stars. In the morning, flip it to the white side, and remember God made everything you see when you walk through the park, go to school, and ride in the car." Grandpa handed little Johnny the picture. With a big smile, little Johnny jumped up and gave his grandpa the biggest hug ever.

"You're the best Grandpa."

Misty eyed Grandpa said, "Now off to bed you go and remember."

"God made everything!"

THE END

Little Johnny
and
God's Breath

Little Johnny was so excited. Grandpa promised that they would roast marshmallows tonight. Of course, Little Johnny hurried to complete his nightly chores, so he could join his grandpa outside.

When little Johnny went outside, he saw his grandpa building the fire in the backyard. Little Johnny sat in the swing porch because he knew the rules. He could hear his grandpa's voice in his head. "Johnny, stay on the porch while I build this fire. I don't want you to get burned. A fire has to be built the safe way. That is far away from any thing that can catch on fire including you, or you don't build it at all."

"Yep," thought Little Johnny, "that's exactly what Grandpa would say."

Coming out of his thoughts, little Johnny noticed that Grandpa first made a circle out of the rocks. Next, he added the kindling, and then, he made a tepee out of some twigs. Grandpa lit the fire and blew it. "Hmm," thought little Johnny, "I never noticed that before." Grandpa added wood and blew some more. The wood softly crackled as it rose to a vibrant orange glow. The more Grandpa blew; the bigger the flame got. "Wow!" thought little Johnny.

As the flame settled down, Grandpa shouted, "Johnny, you can come over now." Jumping off the porch and onto the yard, Johnny ran to his grandpa's side. Johnny got comfortable next to his grandpa, and Grandpa began roasting the marshmallows. Oh, Johnny could hardly wait. He was already licking his lips in anticipation of that gooey-gooey sweet melt-in-your-mouth marshmallow. As Grandpa took the marshmallows off the flame, he noticed little Johnny's brightened facial expression. Grandpa chuckled and handed little Johnny the first roasted marshmallows. Almost immediately, little Johnny dived into the marshmallows with his mouth. Grandpa laughed as little Johnny looked up with marshmallow covering his entire mouth.

As Grandpa began roasting marshmallows for himself, he asked little Johnny what he wanted to talk about. "Hmmm, let me think," said little Johnny. Thinking aloud, "So many things I have questions about, but I don't know where to start."

Laughing, Grandpa said, "Let's start with the last thirty minutes."

"Oh! Oh! Oh! I know."

"What?"

"When you built the fire, you blew on it to make it bigger. Why?"

"That's the way I make it come alive. It's just like God's breath."

"God's breath?"

"Yes. The same way God breathed into man is the same way I breathed on the fire to make it come alive."

"So! You make it come alive when you breathe on it. But, how do you make it die?"

"When we finish roasting marshmallows, I am going to cover the whole fire with that bucket of dirt over there."

"So, dirt makes it dead, but breath made it come alive."

"Exactly."

"So when God made us, he breathed on us, and we came alive. But, when we are not alive we have dirt on us."

"You almost got it. Tomorrow after breakfast, I will show you. Deal?"

"Deal!"

"Okay, let's put this fire out and head to bed, and I will see you at breakfast." Grabbing the bucket of dirt together, Grandpa and little Johnny put the fire out. Then, they headed to the house to have sweet dreams.

All night, little Johnny dreamed about God's breath. And when morning came, he hurriedly brushed his teeth, so he could meet Grandpa downstairs. Bounding down the stairs in excitement, little Johnny could hear the clinking of pots and pans. When he saw Grandpa at the breakfast table, he gave a wide smile of anticipation. "Come on Johnny. Sit down," said Grandpa, "When your grandma is done with breakfast, you and I will get to cook."

"Grandpa, remember you told me I was not allowed near the stove," little Johnny said.

"Well, this will be a little different. I am here to supervise. I will actually place our little project in the oven, but we are going to make it together," said Grandpa, "Now, eat up. We have fun to get to."

Breakfast was so good: Pancakes, eggs, and bacon. Little Johnny loved his grandma's cooking. When they finished breakfast, little Johnny started his morning chores. "Johnny, don't worry about cleaning just yet. Our project may get a little messy. Go get my paper from yesterday. We need that to cover the counter tops and possibly the floor," Grandpa chuckled.

Johnny bounded out the kitchen door in search of yesterday's newspaper. When he returned to the kitchen, Grandpa had set out flour, salt, water, bowls, measuring cups, food coloring, and the step stool. Grandpa took the newspaper from Johnny and spread it on the counter tops and the floor where they would stand.

Grandpa invited little Johnny to join him. Little Johnny stepped up on the stool and looked inquisitively over all the items on the counter. Peering down at little Johnny, Grandpa said, "On the third day, God made every plant and herb in the field, but there was not a man to work the ground, and God had not caused it to rain." Raising his hand, Grandpa loudly whispered, "Instead, a water mist came up out of the earth and watered the whole earth. God formed man on the sixth day so he could tend to the land. He made the man out of the dust of the ground. Dust is like this flour."

Picking up the flour, Grandpa put some in a bowl along with salt and some water. Then, Grandpa mixed in some food coloring. The mixture looked very close to the color of skin. As Little Johnny looked on, Grandpa shaped out a head, eyes, ears, nose, mouth, body, arms, and legs. Little Johnny could hardly believe it. Grandpa made the shape of a man. "When God finished shaping the man, God breathed into the man's nose, and the man came alive. God named the man Adam."

"That's awesome!" little Johnny exclaimed, "Did God make the girl the same way?"

"Well, not quite. After God made Adam come alive, God placed Adam in a garden named Eden and said take care of the garden. Eat off of every tree in the garden except one, the tree of knowledge of good and evil. At some point, God decided that Adam should not be by himself. So, God made Adam a help meet. Before He made Adam a help meet, God brought all the field animals and the birds of the air to Adam to name. But, none of the field animals or birds of the air were a help meet for Adam. When none of the animals or birds was suitable for Adam, God made Adam fall into a deep sleep. When Adam fell asleep, God took out one of Adam's ribs." Grandpa took a piece of dough from the dough Adam's chest.

Little Johnny looked at his stomach. Grandpa continued, "With that rib, God shaped the woman." Handing Johnny Adam's rib, Grandpa said, "Let's make the woman together." Together little Johnny and his grandpa shaped out the woman.

"Don't forget her eyes and nose Grandpa. Oh and she needs arms and legs too. Oh! Oh! Oh! We almost forgot her ears. Grandpa, what about her hair?"

"We will add hair and more color when we finish baking and cooling. That way, everything will stay in place. Johnny, I'm surprised you didn't ask what the woman's name was."

"What did God name the woman?"

"Actually, Adam named the woman. Her name was Eve."

"Eve." Thinking aloud, little Johnny rapidly said, "I think I got the whole story now Grandpa. Adam was the man. Eve was the woman. God made Adam out of dust and blew in his nose, like you blew on the fire, and Adam came alive. Then, God put Adam asleep and took Adam's rib to make the woman, Eve."

"You've got it, Johnny! You're so smart!"

Giving his grandpa a big proud toothy smile, Johnny said "Thanks Grandpa. Can we bake now?"

Chuckling, Grandpa said, "My impatient little Johnny…. Sure, we can start. We need to put wax paper on the cookie sheet so Adam and Eve won't stick. While they cook, we will clean up and get the other supplies to finish decorating them."

"Yes, we need to get them clothes."

Putting his arm around little Johnny's shoulder, Grandpa said, "I will have to tell you about Adam and Eve's clothes later. Uh, it was a different situation from today's time."

THE END

Little Johnny
and the
Football Fiasco

Little Johnny ran inside of the house and threw his backpack on the sofa. "Grandpa, can Bobby and Jimmy come over to play?"

"Johnny, hold on. You know the rules about your backpack."

"Sorry, Grandpa." Little Johnny grabbed his backpack, ran upstairs, and ran back downstairs. "Can they? Can they come and play?"

"Did you do well in school today?"

"Yes, Grandpa."

"Do you have any homework?"

"No, Grandpa."

"Do you have any chores you need to complete?"

"No sir; all done."

"Ok, where are you all going to play?"

"In the back yard….Bobby has his football."

"That's fine, but you all need to play in the open space. You can play anywhere in the open space even by the trees, but do not get in your grandma's flower bed."

"Okay. We won't."

"Go on."

"Thanks, Grandpa!" Little Johnny swung open the front door and shouted, "He said yes. Let's go to the back yard." The boys ran to the backyard excitedly talking about their football moves.

Johnny said, "Okay, this is the plan. We can play in that open space over there, but Grandpa said, we cannot get in the flower bed."

They all agreed, and Bobby said, "I want to throw the ball first." Bobby threw the ball, and Johnny and Jimmy ran to catch it. Jimmy caught it, and Johnny tackled. Then, Jimmy threw the ball, and Johnny tackled Bobby. The boys were having so much fun, but they started to get hot.

Bobby said, "Hey, Jimmy we should throw the ball closer to house where the shade is. I'm getting hot."

Jimmy responded, "No, remember what Johnny's grandpa said. He said we had to play in the open space. If we get by the shade, we're going to get in the flower bed."

Johnny said, "Yeah, we better stay in the open area."

"Okay," Bobby responded.

The boys continued to play, toppling one over the other giggling. "Whew, I'm tired, and I'm really hot," Bobby said.

"Me too," Jimmy agreed.

"Well, we can always go in the house and get some lemonade. I know my grandma has some," said Johnny.

"No," Bobby said, "they'll make us stay inside because it's so hot."

"Yeah, I want to stay outside and play," Jimmy whined.

"You know if we could get in the shaded area just a little bit, we would not be so hot. Don't you think so Jimmy?" Bobby asked.

Jimmy responded, "That's not a bad idea, but we're going to be close to the flowers."

Bobby replied, "It won't be so bad. Look, I'll show you." Bobby jumps up off the ground and runs to the shaded area close to the flowers. "See, it's not so bad. If I stay in this spot, we won't be in the flowers."

"He sounds so convincing Johnny. It doesn't seem that bad really," said Jimmy.

"Well, you have a point," replied Johnny, "maybe just long enough to get cooled off."

Johnny and Jimmy joined Bobby in the shaded area. "Ah, this is nice and cool," said Jimmy."

"See. I told you," said Bobby.

"Here," said Bobby as he tossed the ball to Jimmy.

"Here," said Jimmy as he tossed the ball to Johnny.

Before they knew it, the boys were playing football again but in the shaded area. They were all giggling and having such a good time until Bobby threw the ball too high.

"Oh no!" screamed Johnny. Johnny and Jimmy tried to catch the ball before it went into the window, but they tripped in the flower bed, and the football went crashing through the window. It was too late.

Crash!

Boom!

"Ow!"Grandpa shouted. Johnny knew he was in big trouble.

"Johnny, I'm going home. Can you bring me my football, later?"asked Bobby, as he took off running.

As Grandpa opened the door, he saw Bobby running toward his house. Rubbing his head, Grandpa went straight to the side of the house where the flower bed was. There, he found Johnny and Jimmy trying to hurriedly put the flower bed back together. However, it was no use; the flowers were broken in several places, and some were even crushed. Johnny and Jimmy had flowers sticking to the backs of their shirts and stems were tangled around their shoes.

"I see we have a situation here," said Grandpa. Johnny and Jimmy held their heads down in shame. "This is a real Adam and Eve situation," said Grandpa, "but just like them you will have to deal with the consequences."

"But it wasn't our fault," Jimmy offered, "We got hot, and Bobby said we would be cooler if we played in the shaded area."

"Bobby said," Grandpa repeated, "Like, I said a real Adam and Eve situation. And Johnny, what's your response?"

So ashamed, Johnny could barely look at his grandpa's face. "Grandpa, it's like Jimmy said."

"And what did I say?" asked Grandpa.

"Play anywhere in the open space, but not by the flower bed," little Johnny said shamefully.

"That's right, but it's okay," said Grandpa. Little Johnny looked up hopefully until Grandpa said, "You both will be responsible for paying and cleaning up this mess. And Bobby cannot come back over. He's a bad influence. I'm going to call your parents Jimmy. Come on inside."

Johnny and Jimmy followed Grandpa inside the house. They anxiously watched as Grandpa called Jimmy's parents and relayed the whole mess. Johnny and Jimmy couldn't say a word. There was nothing to say. They had disobeyed, and Grandpa was very unhappy. And when little Johnny's grandma got home from shopping, there would be more unhappiness. "We shouldn't have listened to Bobby," Johnny whispered.

"You're right," Jimmy whispered back, "Do you know how we're going to be punished?"

"I'm not sure," Johnny whispered, "but I'm sure we will not like it."

Grandpa put down the phone and said, "That's settled. Johnny and Jimmy you will work off the money that it is going to take to repair the flower bed and the window. The total cost is going to be about $150."

"$150!" Johnny and Jimmy exclaimed.

"But we don't have any money Grandpa," said little Johnny.

"How are we ever going to pay?" said Jimmy, throwing his hands in the air. "We're not old enough to work! I only have $5 that I got for my birthday!"

"Like I said before, this is a real Adam and Eve situation," Grandpa repeated, folding his arms on his chest.

"What do you mean, Grandpa?" asked little Johnny.

"Sit down, and I will tell you the story. God made a beautiful garden named Eden for Adam and Eve to live in. God told Adam that he could eat off of every tree in the garden except the tree of knowledge of good and evil, which is in the midst of the garden. One day, a snake approached Eve. The snake told Eve she could eat off the tree of knowledge of good and evil, which was in the midst of the garden. Eve told the snake that God said they were not to eat off the tree or they would die. The snake told Eve 'you are not going to die, but you and Adam will be as gods knowing good and evil.' Eve looked at the tree, saw that it was good for food, saw that it was nice to look at, and thought it would make her smart. Eve ate the fruit off the tree. Then, Eve gave some to Adam. Now, Adam and Eve knew things that would be bad for them. God was very unhappy with them. When God asked Adam and Eve what happened, Adam blamed Eve, and Eve blamed the snake. God punished Adam and Eve by putting them out of beautiful Eden. God decided that Adam would work hard for his food, and Eve would have a hard time with their children. Also, Adam and Eve would no longer live forever. God said Adam and Eve would return to dust. And just like God said eventually Adam and Eve stopped living."

"That's bad, Grandpa. Really, really bad," said Johnny, "I'm sorry we were disobedient."

"Me too," Jimmy said sadly.

"See; it doesn't feel good when you are disobedient. Everyone has sad faces," said Grandpa.

"We won't do it again Grandpa. I promise," little Johnny said.

"Me too," said Jimmy.

"I'm sure you won't, but you still have to pay back the money. For the next three weeks you two will be doing extra chores and have no television or video game privileges." Johnny and Jimmy both looked really sad.

For the next three weeks, little Johnny and Jimmy were on their best behavior. Whatever they were asked or told to do, they did it without hesitation. After the three-week punishment, they were tired, but happy with themselves. They both knew that they would never listen to friends like Bobby again, and their grandparents and parents were no longer sad with them. They had learned their lesson.

THE END

Little Johnny
and the
Big Gold Star

Little Johnny stomped in the house after school. Little Johnny stomped up the stairs and put his backpack up. Little Johnny stomped back downstairs for his afternoon snack.

"Hey buddy," Grandpa said, "why the long face? Come sit next to me on the sofa and tell me about it."

"Today was the worst day ever at school," said little Johnny, as he sat next to his grandpa.

"And why is that?" Grandpa questioned.

"Because…I didn't get a prize, and I couldn't play outside," pouted Johnny, "so unfair."

"Unfair, huh. Tell me what happened."

"Well, Jimmy and I were hoping to get the big gold star. Our teacher said whoever finished the assignment first would be the winner of the big gold star. So, I hurried up and finished first except Jimmy and I finished at the same time, so the teacher had to decide who would get the prize. She gave it to Jimmy and not me. Jimmy was happy, but I was mad."

"Why did the teacher choose Jimmy's and not yours?" asked Grandpa.

"She said I didn't do my best work. She said that it was messy, and I didn't do it quite as instructed."

"And Jimmy's, how was his work?"

"It was neat, and he did everything just as the teacher said."

"Uh huh. So, you know why you didn't get the big gold star. Why couldn't you go outside and play."

"I was just so mad. Jimmy was all happy. I know he's my best friend or used to be, but I was so mad. So when I went back to my seat, I pushed Jimmy."

"Johnny," Grandpa said with a disapproving and disappointed voice, "I see, and how did Jimmy feel about that?"

Looking ashamed, Johnny said, "He was mad. When I pushed him, I didn't know he was going to fall and hit his lip."

"Johnny!" exclaimed Grandpa. "You are in trouble! Why didn't the school call us?"

"Because Jimmy didn't want me to get in trouble....He told the teacher it was okay that he understood why I did it, but the teacher still punished me. No recess for three whole days."

"You better be glad that's the only thing you got."

"I'm sorry Grandpa. I don't know what happened. Jimmy's my best friend or used to be, but I was just so mad."

"I think there are two lessons to be learned here Johnny. One is you have to always give your best. If you give your best, you don't have to worry about being so mad. Two is you have to learn how to deal with your anger in the right way. This reminds me of the brothers Cain and Abel."

"Cain and Abel?"

"Yes, Cain and Abel were two sons of Adam and Eve. You remember Adam and Eve, right?"

"Yes, of course. Adam and Eve were the first two people on Earth, and the first two people to sin."

"Right. Well, Adam and Eve had two sons named Cain and Abel. When Cain grew up, he became a farmer. But when Abel grew up, he became a shepherd or someone who takes care of sheep. One day when the farm was lush and the sheep were big, Cain and Abel brought an offering to God. Cain brought some of the vegetables from the farm, and Abel brought the biggest and best sheep. When God saw Abel's offering, He was very pleased. When God saw Cain's offering, He was displeased. Cain was disappointed and became very angry. God asked Cain, 'Why are you mad? Why are you disappointed?' God went on to say to Cain, 'that if you don't do well, sin is waiting at the door.' That means that when you are mad and not thinking straight you can do bad things."

"Did Cain do something bad?" asked little Johnny.

"Matter of fact, he did. Cain and his brother Abel were talking in the field when Cain took his brother's life."

"Oh no, Grandpa! I would never do that to Jimmy. He's my friend."

"Would you have thought you would have pushed Jimmy?" asked Grandpa.

"Of course not! I was just mad," responded little Johnny.

"Cain was just mad too, but you don't have to stay mad. There are some things you can do to help you deal with being mad."

"How?" little Johnny asked curiously.

"You can say a prayer. You can walk away. You can count numbers. Or you could have congratulated your friend Jimmy and did better the next time."

"I should have congratulated Jimmy and did better next time. I got to tell Jimmy I'm sorry Grandpa. Can I call him on the phone?"

"Sure Johnny. Go do it."

Little Johnny jumped off the sofa and called Jimmy and apologized. He was so happy to be friends with Jimmy again, and they made plans to play baseball the following weekend. When little Johnny got to school the next day, he asked his teacher if he could redo the assignment while the other children played during recess. Little Johnny's teacher agreed. Little Johnny did his very best, and the teacher was proud. The teacher put a small gold star on little Johnny's paper. He was so proud. It turned out okay. Little Johnny now knew that he must always do his best, and he won't be so mad. And if he did get mad, he knew he could pray, be nice, walk away, or even count numbers. Little Johnny was proud of himself.

THE END

Bible Study Lessons

Dear Lesson Leader,

Thank you once again for making a difference in a child's life. Each lesson that follows is designed for a fifty minute to one hour class period. Prior to teaching, take time to pray and prepare. Allow the Holy Spirit to lead you, and enjoy the experience.

Suggested Class Format
1. Have a devotional.
    a. Sing a favorite children's church song.
    b. Ask children for concerns or prayer request.
    c. Say a prayer with the children.
2. Start lesson!
3. Review! Review! Review!
4. After the lesson, allow children to have social time.

LESSON 1:
GOD CREATED EVERYTHING

Lesson Goal: To teach that God created everything

Scripture Reference: Genesis 1 – 2:3

Basic List of Materials
1. White Construction Paper
2. Black Construction Paper
3. Glue/ Glue stick
4. Crayons
5. Single Hole puncher
6. String

Optional Materials to Add to the Fun
1. Markers
2. Paint
3. Glitter
4. Precut shapes

Lesson Story/Activity
   Instructions: As the lesson leader vividly tells the story, the lesson leader will act out the story. The parentheses that follow

the sentences are expected answers from the children or expected actions from the lesson leader. The children will repeat the creation process during the activity portion.

Who do you think created the world? (Allow the children to answer freely)

In the beginning, God created the heavens and the earth. And darkness was in the deep. (Show black piece of paper)

God said, "let there be light." (Show white piece of paper)

And there was light. God saw that the light was a good thing. God divided the light from the darkness. (Glue black & white together)

What do you think God called the light? (Day)

What do you think God called the dark? (Night)

And the evening and the morning were the first day. Now, water covered the entire Earth. So, God decided to divide the water. God placed some water up top and some water on the bottom. Do you know how God divided the water at the top from the water at the bottom? (Various answers)

God placed Heaven in between. (Place clouds on white side)

And the evening and the morning were the second day. Next God said let all the water under Heaven be in one place and let the dry land appear. And it happened. God called the dry land Earth. God called all the gathered water Seas. (On the white side about a ¼ up from the bottom of the page, place the brown land 2/3 across, and draw the sea over the remaining 1/3.)

And God saw that it was what? (A good thing)

God saw that it was a good thing but God did not stop there. God said to the earth "Earth, bring forth grass, flowers, & fruit trees." And the Earth did. (Add a few items to the white side)

What kind of trees do you think the Earth brought forth? (Various answers)

And God saw that it was what? (A good thing)

God saw that it was a good thing. And the evening and the morning were the third day. Now God had created the Earth, Heaven, trees, and seas. But there were some things still missing. What tells us when it is the day time? (Sun) (Place Sun on white side)

What tells us when it is night time? (Moon and Stars) (Place moon and stars on the black side)

God did this so we could have signs, seasons, days, and years. And God saw that it was what? (A good thing) God saw that it was a good thing. And the evening and morning were the fourth day.

Do you think God was done yet? There were some things still missing. God told the waters to bring forth the fish, great whales, and the other sea animals. Also, God created the birds to fly in Heaven. (Place a bird and a sea animal in the appropriate places)

And the evening and morning were the fifth day. After creating the birds and fish, God still was not done. Next God created some oink oinks, woof woofs, moo moos, and some roars. What animal says oink oink? (Pig)

What says woof woof? (Dog)

What says moo moo? (Cow)

What says roar? (Tigers, bears, lions, etc.) (Place an animal on the white side)

And God saw that it was a what? (A good thing)

But you know what? God still was not done. He had one more very special project to do. So God said, "Come on Jesus. Come on Holy Spirit. Let's make man in our own image." So God made a man and a woman. (Place man and woman on the white side)

Finally, God saw everything He had made, and it was a very good thing. And the evening and the morning were the sixth day. On the seventh day, God rested and sanctified it. Now, it's your turn to reenact.

Instructions: *Activity time! The student (s) will reenact/ draw the Creation as you read.*

To each child, pass out a piece of white paper, a piece of black paper, glue, and drawing utensils. Let the students freely think with their colors. This activity will take some time depending on the age of the children present. Invite others to assist in helping the children. Enjoy!

1. On the first day, God made the light and separated it from the darkness. Glue white and black pieces of paper together.
2. On the second day, God made the heavens. Place clouds on top of the white paper.
3. On the third day, God gathered the water to make the Sea and revealed the land underneath. At the bottom of the white paper, place land and sea. Then the Earth brought forth grass, flowers, and fruit trees. Place grass, a flower, and a tree.
4. On the fourth day, God made the Sun, the moon, and the stars. Place Sun at the top of white side. Place moon and lots of stars on the black side. (Recommend using white or yellow so moon and stars will really shine)
5. On the fifth day, God created the birds and told the water to bring forth fish. On the white side, place birds (wide "m" shape) in the sky and a fish or sea creature in the sea.
6. On the sixth day, God made other animals and man. On the white paper, draw your favorite animal. Then, draw a man and a woman.

7. On the seventh day, God rested and made that day holy.
8. On the black side, write "The Creation". Punch hole in the middle of artwork, and place string through the hole for hanging.

**Suggestion: Have children to hang the picture on their bedroom door knob. Tell the children to turn the picture to the white side when it's day and the black side when it's night. The children will be constantly reminded that God created everything. **

Lesson 1 Review Questions

1. In the beginning, who created the heavens and the earth? (God)
2. Who created the light? (God)
3. Who created the sky? (God)
4. What tells us when it is day? (Sun)
5. Who made the Sun? (God)
6. What tells us when it is night? (Stars and moon)
7. Who made the stars and moon? (God)
8. Who made the trees and the sea? (God)
9. Who made the fish in the sea and the birds in the air? (God)
10. What says woof woof? (Dog)
11. Who made the dog? (God)
12. What says oink oink? (Pig)
13. Who made the pig? (God)
14. What says roar? (Tigers, Lions, Bears, etc.)
15. Who made them? (God)
16. Who made man? (God)
17. Who made woman? (God)
18. Who made everything? (God)

Jacqui Wilson

LESSON 2:
GOD CREATED ADAM AND EVE

Lesson Goal: To teach how God created Adam and Eve
Scripture Reference: Genesis 2:4-7; 18-25
Basic List of Materials

1. Aprons or old clothing
2. Newspaper
3. Flour
4. Salt
5. Water
6. Bowls
7. Measuring cup
8. Cookie sheets
9. Wax paper
10. Pre-heated 450 degree Oven

Optional Materials to Add to the Fun

1. Food coloring
2. Paint (to decorate post-baking)
3. Craft eyes (to decorate pre-baking)
4. Yarn (use post-baking)
5. Glue (use post-baking)

Play Dough Recipe (Should create four people)

1. Mix together 1 cup of flour, ½ cup salt, and ½ cup water
2. If sticky, add more flour.
3. Add food coloring to change pigment (optional)

Lesson Story/Activity

Instructions: Pre-make one play dough recipe. Then, tell the story of how God made Adam and Eve. Act out the story.

On the third day, God made every plant and herb in the field. There was not a man to work the ground, and God had not caused it to rain. Instead, a water mist came up out of the earth and watered the whole earth. On the sixth day, God formed man out of the dust of the ground. Do you know what dust is? Dust is like this flour. God took the dust and formed the man. (Place some dust (flour) on the pre-made play dough and form a man as you talk)

What do you think God gave the man? (Head, eyes, ears, nose, mouth, body, arms, legs, etc.)

When God finish shaping the man, God breathed into the man's nose and the man came alive. Wow! Can you believe that? God named the man Adam.

1. Activity time! Let each of the children make an Adam out of play dough.
2. After each child has made an Adam, tell the children to take a piece of Adam from his chest section and set it aside.
3. *Optional: Bake the Adams for 15 minutes at 450 degrees so the Adams can harden like a biscuit. (You can make the play dough edible.)
4. Tell the rest of the story.

After God made Adam come alive, God placed Adam in a garden named Eden and said take care of the garden. Eat off of every tree in the garden except one, the tree of knowledge of good and evil.

At some point, God decided that Adam should not be by himself. Do you like being by yourself all the time? All of us like to have a friend at least. So, God decided to make Adam a help meet. God brought all the field animals and birds of the air to Adam to name. But, none of the field animals or birds of the air were a help meet for Adam. When none of the animals or birds was suitable for Adam, God made Adam fall into a deep sleep. When Adam fell asleep, God took out one of Adam's ribs. Where is your rib? Remember the piece you took out of your play dough Adam. God took Adam's rib and made a woman. Adam named the woman Eve.

1. Activity time! Let each child form a play dough woman. Tell the children to start with Adam's rib. ***Don't forget to take Adam out of the oven and let him cool. ***
2. Optional: Bake Eve while you decorate Adam or review questions.
3. Everyone clean up together. Sing a fun song.
4. Social/play time until Eve finishes baking and cooling. Then, decorate!

Lesson 2 Review Questions
1. Who made man? (God)
2. What did God make the man from? (Dust of the ground)
3. How did God make the man come alive? (Blew in his nose)
4. What did God name the man? (Adam)
5. Why did God make the man? (To take care of the garden)

6. What was the name of the garden? (Eden)
7. Who took care of the garden before Adam? (Water mist from God)
8. Who named the field animals and birds? (Adam)
9. What did Adam name the field animals and birds? (Various answers)
10. Did the field animals and birds look like Adam? (No)
11. What is the opposite of a man or a boy? (Woman or girl)
12. Who made woman? (God)
13. How did God make the woman? (Adam's rib)
14. What was the woman's name? (Eve)
15. Who named the woman? (Adam)
16. So who created man? (God)
17. Who created woman? (God)
18. Who created you and me? (God)
19. Who created mommies and daddies? (God)
20. Who created brothers, sisters, cousin, aunts, uncles, and everyone you know? (God)
21. Who created everything? (God)

LESSON 3:
HAPPY FACE OR SAD FACE

Lesson Goal: To teach consequences of disobedience

Scripture Reference: Genesis 2:8-9, 15-17; 3:1-23

Basic List of Materials
1. Construction paper
2. Scissors
3. Popsicle or lollipop stick(s)
4. Glue
5. Drying surface such as a table

Lesson Story/Activity
1. Each student should make a happy/sad face on the stick prior to the lesson story.
2. Allow each student to choose two different colors of construction paper. Place the two pieces of construction paper back to back and cut a large circle out of both. (You can precut all the circles)
3. Give the student(s) the two circles. On one circle the student is to make a happy face. On the other circle the student is to make a sad face.

4. Place one circle face down on a drying surface. On the non-face side of that circle, place glue all the way around approximately 1/8 to 1/4 of an inch away from the edge.
5. Place popsicle/craft stick up to halfway on the wet glue side of the circle. Then press other faced circle on top. (*Make sure faces are positioned the same way.)
6. Write child's name on the stick vertically.
7. To make it more fun, the student(s) can always add hair, eyes that move, etc.
8. When the project dries, the student should be able to flip the stick to see a happy face on one side and a sad face on the other side.

God made a beautiful garden named Eden for Adam and Eve to live. God told Adam that he could eat off of every tree in the garden except one. What did God tell Adam? (Allow student to answer)

What did God tell Adam? (Allow student to answer again)

God said Adam you can eat off of every tree except the tree of knowledge of good and evil in the midst of the garden. What was the name of the tree? (Allow student to answer)

God said Adam don't eat off the tree of knowledge of good and evil in the midst of the garden.

One day, a snake approached Eve. The snake told Eve she could eat off the tree of knowledge of good and evil in the midst of the garden. What did God tell Adam? Do you think God wanted Eve to eat off the tree of knowledge of good and evil if God told Adam not to eat off of it? (Allow student to answer)

Eve told the snake that God said that they were not to eat off the tree or they would die. Has someone ever told you not to do something because something bad would happen? (Allow student to answer)

The snake told Eve you are not going to die, but you and Adam will be as gods knowing good and evil.

Now, would you have a conversation with a snake? (Allow student to answer)

What should Eve have done when the snake started talking to her? (Walked away)

But do you know what Eve did? Eve looked at the tree, saw that it was good for food, saw that it was nice to look at, and thought it would make her smart. Just because something looks good or tastes good does not mean it is good for you. What is your favorite food? (Allow student to answer) It smells so yummy and tastes so good. What if your mom says don't eat that tonight? Would you still eat it? (Allow student to answer)

What if mom said don't eat that tonight because it has poison in it? Would you eat it? (Allow student to answer)

If God tells you not to do something, it is for a good reason even if you don't understand.

Do you know what Eve did? Eve ate the fruit off the tree of knowledge of good and evil, which was in the midst of the garden. Then, Eve gave some fruit from the tree to Adam. Adam and Eve sinned when they were disobedient to God. Sin is when you do something bad.

If you had a friend who told you to do something that your parents told you not to do, would you do it? (Allow student to answer)

If your mom said I don't want you to ride your bike on the rocky path but your friend said come on I have done it lots of time, would you do it? (Allow student to answer)

What if you fall and cut yourself on the rocks or bust your bike tire? Is that a good thing or bad thing? (It's a bad thing)

What does the word disobedient mean? (Allow student to answer)

Disobedient means to do something you are not supposed to do or a bad thing. Adam and Eve were disobedient. God punished Adam and Eve by kicking them out of the beautiful Garden of Eden. Also, God made Adam work hard for his food, and Eve had a hard time with her children.

Do you think God had a sad face or a happy face when he put Adam and Eve out of the garden? (Sad face)

Do you think Adam and Eve had a happy or sad face when God put them out of the garden? (Sad face)

If you were Adam and Eve, would you have a happy face of sad face if God was unhappy with you? (Sad face)

Another punishment God gave Adam and Eve was death. God said Adam and Eve would return to dust, which is to die.

Activity Time!

Instructions: Tell student(s) to retrieve his/her face on the stick. You will ask the student the questions below. The student will then show a happy face or sad face to indicate the consequence for each action. Discuss consequences of each act. Feel free to add more questions. Have fun!

1. Do you like getting happy faces?
2. When you do something good, do you get a happy face or sad face?
3. When you do something bad, do you get a happy face or a sad face?
4. You pick up your toys when mom says pick up your toys. Happy face or sad face? (Happy face)
5. You eat all the food on your plate. Happy face or sad face? (Happy face)
6. You do what your teacher tells you to do? Happy face or sad face? (Happy face)
7. You say a bad word. Happy face or sad face? (Sad face)
8. You hit another child because you are being mean. Happy face or sad face? (Sad face)
9. You give someone a hug. (Happy face)
10. You tell your friend you cannot go outside because your mom said not to go outside. (Happy face)
11. You spit on someone. (Sad face)
12. You make a good grade. (Happy face)
13. You help your mom. (Happy face)

14. You take something that does not belong to you. (Sad face)
15. You run in the street when your mom said don't. (Sad face)
16. You do what God tells you to do. (Happy face)

Lesson 3 Review Questions

1. What was the name of the garden Adam and Eve lived in? (Eden)
2. What did God tell Adam not to do? (Don't eat off the fruit tree in the midst of the garden or don't eat off the tree of knowledge of good and evil)
3. Did Adam eat off the tree God told him not to eat off of? (Yes)
4. Who gave Adam the fruit? (Eve)
5. Was that a good thing or bad thing? (Bad thing)
6. Who told Eve it was okay for her to eat the fruit? (A snake)
7. Was that a good thing or bad thing? (Bad thing)
8. Why did Eve listen to the snake? (Various answers – fruit look good, so she could be smart, etc.)
9. Does it matter why Eve ate the fruit? (No)
10. Why doesn't it matter why Eve ate the fruit? (Because God told them not to eat it)
11. Do you think God had a happy face or sad face when Adam and Eve ate the fruit? (Sad face)
12. When you do something that you are not suppose to do, do you get punished? (Yes)
13. Did God punish Adam and Eve? (Yes)
14. How did God punish Adam and Eve? (God put Adam and Eve out of the Garden of Eden. Adam

had to work hard. Eve had a hard time with her children. Adam and Eve would return to the dust (die).)

15. What is sin? (Doing a bad thing)
16. What kind of face do you get if you sin? (Sad face)
17. Who were the first people to sin? (Adam and Eve)
18. Are you going to try to get happy faces or sad faces? (Happy faces)
19. Who gives you a happy face when you do right or good things? (God, parents, teacher, etc.)

LESSON 4:
GOD WANTS YOUR BEST

Lesson Goal: To give God your best

Scripture Reference: Genesis 4:1-5

Basic List of Materials
1. Paper
2. Crayons
3. Hole puncher
4. String

Lesson Story
1. When someone says (child's name) you are the best ever, how does that make you feel?
2. When someone gives you a gift that you really want, how does that make you feel?
3. I have two cookies. One is big and has all your favorite things in it. One is broken into pieces and only has a few of the things you like. Which one do you want? Why?
4. There are two bikes in the yard. One is kind of rusty and missing some paint. The other bike is a brand new shiny red bike. Which one do you want? Why?

5. (To a girl) I have two dolls. One is a regular doll and the other is a princess doll. Which one would you like? Why?

6. (To a boy) I have two video games. One video game is the old version, and one is the new version? Which one would you like? Why?

7. Let's pretend like God is sitting right here with us. You have two sandwiches. One sandwich you have taken a bite of, and the other sandwich you have not eaten off of. Which sandwich would you give to God? Why?

8. Let's pretend I have your favorite sandwich. I split the sandwich in three pieces, but one piece is bigger than all the others. Would you want the big piece, or would you give the big piece to someone else?

9. Let's say one of your friends come over to play. Would you let your friend play with your favorite toy? Discuss.

I want to tell you a story about two brothers. One was named Cain and the other Abel. Cain and Abel were the sons of Adam and Eve. When Cain grew up, he became a farmer. What are some of your favorite things that farmers grow? (Various answers)

But when Abel grew up, he became a shepherd or someone who takes care of sheep. What is a shepherd? What sound do sheep make? (Baaaa)

One day when the farm was lush and the sheep were big, Cain and Abel brought an offering to God. Cain brought some of the vegetables from the farm to God. And Abel brought the biggest and best sheep to God. When God saw Abel's offering, He was very pleased. Why do you think God was happy with Abel's offering? Discuss.

When God saw Cain's offering, He was displeased. Why do you think God was unhappy with Cain's offering? Discuss.

When God was displeased with Cain's offering Cain was very mad. Should Cain have been mad? Discuss.

Lesson 4 Review Questions:
1. What were the two brothers' names? (Cain and Abel)
2. What was Cain? (Farmer)
3. What kind of things do farmers grow? (Various answers)
4. What was Abel? (Shepherd)
5. What does a shepherd do? (take care of sheep)
6. Who gave their best to God? (Abel)
7. How did God feel about Abel's offering? (happy)
8. How did God feel about Cain's offering? (unhappy)
9. How did Cain feel when God was unhappy with his offering? (Sad, Mad, etc.)
10. What is the best thing you can do? (Individually answers)
11. Are you willing to give your best to God? (Yes)
12. Do you do your best at school? (Various answers)
13. Are you on your best behavior all the time? (Various answers)
14. If someone asks you to sing a song, will you do your best? (Yes)
15. If God asked you for a cookie, would you give God a broken cookie? (No)
16. How do you feel when someone says you are the best? (Good)

17. How do you think God feels when you do your best? (Good)
18. Don't you want God to feel happy and good all the time? (Yes)

So give your best!

Activity

1. Gather enough drawing paper for each child.
2. On the top of the paper, write "To God from (child's name). This is my best."
3. Below draw a large square/rectangle (big enough to draw or paint a picture)
4. Tell the children to draw, paint, etc. their best picture or favorite thing in the square.
5. On the blank side of the paper, you or the student will place a big smiley face. (Can be done prior depending on whether you use crayons/markers/paint)
6. After the pictures are completed, tell the students these four things.
   a. God always gives you the best. Look at everything we have. He gave us the whole world.
   b. Because you have given your best, God is happy. (Flip to smiley face.)
   c. Every time you do your best, God is happy.
   d. When you have done your best, look at the picture, and see God smiling at you because you have done your best.
7. Punch a hole at the top of each picture. Place string through the hole for the children to hang at home.

8. While the children complete this activity, review questions from this lesson.

LESSON 5:
BE MAD, BUT DON'T DO WRONG

Lesson Goal: To teach how to deal with anger

Scripture Reference: Genesis 4:1-16

Basic List of Materials
1. 8 ½ x 11 Construction Paper (1 piece for each child. Avoid dark colors.)
2. 8 ½ x 11 White printer paper
3. Crayons
4. Markers (optional because may bleed through the paper depending on weight)
5. Magazine pictures (optional)
6. Glue (optional)
7. Hole puncher
8. Colorful String or yarn

Discussion:
1. How do you look when you get mad?
2. What are some things that make you mad?
3. What do you do when you get mad?

Lesson Story

Instructions: Retell Lesson 4 story. Then, follow with the rest of this story.

Cain stayed mad. He did not try to do better. Instead, Cain took his brother's life while they were in the field talking. God asked Cain where Abel was, but Cain pretended like he didn't know. Yet, God knew and punished Cain for this sin. What could Cain have done differently? Discuss.

We are going to make a book about the things you can do when you get mad.

1. Each child will need to pick out one piece of colorful construction paper and four pages of white printer paper.

2. Place the white printer paper on top of the construction paper.

3. Fold all pages in half so that the construction paper is the first page and the last page. (Some children may need help.)

4. You will need to place two single-hole punches near the edge of the booklets to help create a binder. The holes should be at least an inch apart. You will then help the children tie one piece of colorful string or yarn through each hole. This will help the book stay in place.

5. Now, the fun part.

   a. On the front, the children should write "My Story" by (child's name).

   b. On the first white page, child should write or draw his/her name.

   c. On the second white page, child should write "When I get mad, I look like this…."

d. On the third white page, child should draw a picture of how they look when they get mad.

e. On the fourth white page, child should write "But I don't stay mad, I…."

f. On the fifth and following white pages, child should draw or pick pictures (to glue) that demonstrate anti-mad acts that they would want to do such as:

Praying (ex. trace hand)

Loving act (ex. heart)

Walking away (ex. legs)

Counting numbers (ex.1-10)

Singing (ex. music notes)

Playing (ex. swing)

Drawing (ex. pencil)

Reading (ex bible)

Tell someone (ex. mouth)

g. Every child should have at least three to four anti-mad acts in their book.

h. When the children are finish, give the children some sample scenarios, so they can practice their anti-mad acts.

Example: Susie doesn't want to play with her friend Sky, but they always play together. Sky becomes mad. What can Sky do? (Sky can go play with someone else for the day, etc.)

Example: Dominic snatched Levi's toy from his hand. What can Levi do? (Tell someone, let Dominic play with the toy, walk away, count numbers, etc.)

Little Johnny's Faith Adventures: Our Beginnings is the first in a series of books that teaches children foundational biblical principles using everyday life situations and interactive lessons. My goal is to help parents and bible study teachers teach God's word to children ages seven and below in a fun and creative manner. This book contains four stories about the daily adventures of Little Johnny followed by five bible study lessons, which can be taught in a classroom setting. Parents or teachers have the option of simply reading the stories about Little Johnny or teaching the lessons that little Johnny has learned. However, the two may be combined to get the most out of the book. Proverbs 22:6 says, "Train up a child in the way he should go: and when he is old, he will not depart from it." As a parent or teacher, this is the best investment you can ever make in a child's life. So, join Little Johnny today as he learns about God's Word. The stories and lessons in this book are based upon Genesis 1-4.

ABOUT THE AUTHOR

A native of Columbus, Ms, Jacqui Wilson grew up the second oldest of seven children. She is an attorney who enjoys writing poetry, singing, and cooking. Currently, she lives in Nashville, TN and attends Rockland M. B. Church in Hendersonville, TN. Jacqui's goal in life is to live within the will of God, fulfilling His purpose for her life.